My Advent

Learn all about Advent with

George & Angie Allen

kevin
mayhew

Advent is . . .

Coming

The word Advent means 'coming'.
During Advent Christians think
about the coming of Jesus
and on Christmas Day
they celebrate his birth.
But Jesus promised he
would come again and
this promise is at the
heart of Advent.

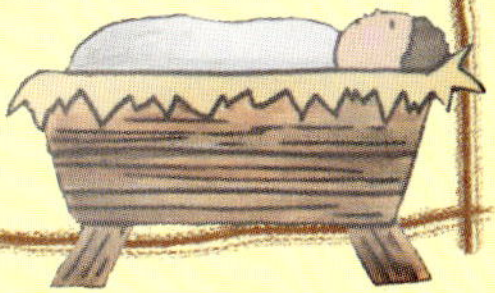

Advent is . . .

Loving

At the beginning of Advent
many churches and homes are
decorated with an Advent Wreath.
It is made of a circle of
evergreen leaves with five
coloured candles.
The circle is like the
love of God; it has no
beginning and no end.

Advent is . . .

Hoping

One of the traditions of Advent is called 'greening'. Green plants like holly and ivy are brought into the house and used as decoration. They are a sign of hope that out of the cold, dark, deadness of winter, new life will come. They are also a reminder that the new life that Jesus brings, like the leaves of the evergreen, is life everlasting.

Advent is . . .

Watching

Jesus is coming!

Jesus didn't tell us when
he would come again. No one, except God,
knows the day or the hour.

But, he did tell us
to always watch and to be
ready so that we are
not taken by surprise.

Advent is . . .

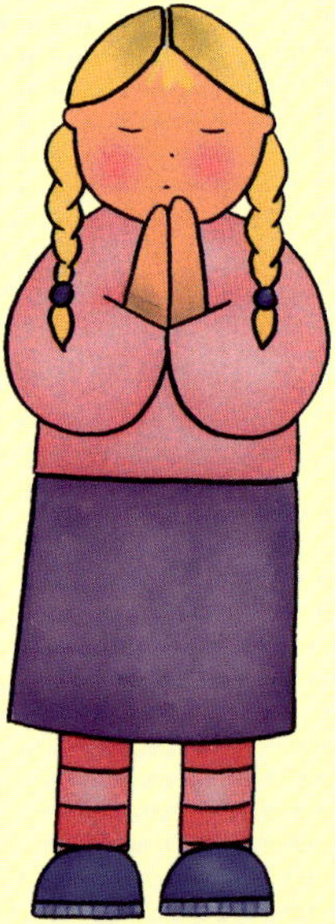

Waiting

Jesus said we should prayerfully wait for him.

We need to be very patient, just like

Simeon in the Bible. Simeon spent the

whole of his life waiting for Jesus to be born.

When he eventually held Jesus in his arms,

he thanked God and felt that his

whole life was complete.

Advent is waiting for Jesus to come

to us again and to make us complete.

Advent is . . .

Seeing

Advent is a season that is full
of light. Houses are decorated inside
and out with coloured lights and candles,
and town centres put on special displays.
We need light to show us the
right path when it is dark.
The Bible teaches us that Jesus is
like a light in the darkness showing us
the way to live our lives.

Advent is . . .

Holding

A Christingle is a specially decorated Christmas orange. The word 'Christingle' probably means 'Christ-light' and it represents a gift given by God for us to hold and to share. The orange represents the world and the sweets on the sticks the earth's resources; the red band recalls Jesus' death on the cross and the candle is a sign that Jesus is the light of the world.

Advent is . . .

Peacemaking

The Prophet Isaiah calls Jesus the Prince of Peace (Isaiah 9:6). When he was on earth Jesus brought peace to people's lives, particularly when they were ill or frightened. Christians believe that when Jesus comes again he will bring peace to the whole earth. There will not be any more wars, and fighting between people will come to an end.

Advent is . . .

Promising

When Jesus comes again he will make everything new in heaven and on earth. He will take away all suffering and pain. There will be no more hunger or thirst. Death will no longer separate us from people we love. There will be no more mourning, and every tear will be dried by God himself.

Advent is . . .

Sharing

Christmas trees are placed in many homes at Christmas. The tradition was started by Martin Luther, a monk who lived in the 16th century. He was walking through a forest and was so overcome by the beauty of the stars twinkling through the branches that he wanted to show his family what it was like. He cut down a small fir tree, took it indoors, and decorated it with lighted candles.

Advent is . . .

Repenting

Different colours are used in church at Advent. Each colour tells a story. Blue or purple is the colour of penitence, reminding us of the need for sorrow before God. It is also the colour of royalty and speaks of Jesus the King. Pink is the colour for celebration and the pink candle is usually lit on Gaudete Sunday. 'Gaudete' is a Latin word for 'rejoice'. White is the colour of purity and reminds us of Jesus.

Advent is . . .

Anticipating

The blue and pink candles in the Advent Wreath are lit, one by one, on the four Sundays of Advent. The flame of each new candle is a reminder that something is happening; God's will is unfolding and there is yet more to come. The light of the white candle says that all will be complete when Jesus has come again.

Advent is . . .

Accepting

When an angel told Mary that she
was to be the mother of Jesus,
the Son of God, by the power of
the Holy Spirit, she accepted without
question that it would happen.
She did not resist the call of God.
She said to the angel,
'Behold, I am the handmaid of the Lord;
let it be to me according to your word.'

Advent is . . .

Expecting

When a woman is going to have a baby, she is often described as 'expecting'. An angel visited Mary, the mother of Jesus, to tell her that God had chosen her out of all the women in the world to be a special servant. She would be with child through the Holy Spirit and bring Jesus into the world.

Advent is . . .

Rejoicing

When a woman knows that she is going to have a baby, she is very excited and loves to tell people. Before Jesus was born Mary went to see her cousin Elizabeth to share her happy news. It was a special meeting because Elizabeth was going to have a baby too, and when Mary walked into the room, Elizabeth's baby jumped for joy. It was the first meeting between John the Baptist and Jesus.

Advent is . . .

Dreaming

Joseph was unhappy when he found that Mary was pregnant because he knew that the baby was not his. One night, he went to bed and had a strange dream. An angel came to him and told him not to be frightened because God was the father of Mary's baby. The angel told Joseph that when the baby was born he was to call him Jesus.

The name Jesus means 'Saviour'.

Advent is . . .

Trusting

Joseph discovered that Mary was going to have a baby before he married her. Instead of breaking off their engagement, he trusted what God had said through an angel about the baby, and he took Mary as his wife. God trusted Joseph to be faithful and to comfort and love Mary as she carried his Son within her.

Advent is . . .

Obeying

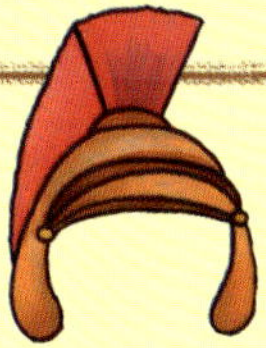

Rome was the ruling power at the time of Jesus' birth, and an order went out from Caesar Augustus that everyone in the Empire had to be counted. To do this, people had to return to their own city. Joseph belonged to Bethlehem, and so, in spite of Mary's advanced stage of pregnancy, they had to make the journey of about seventy miles to be counted.

Advent is . . .

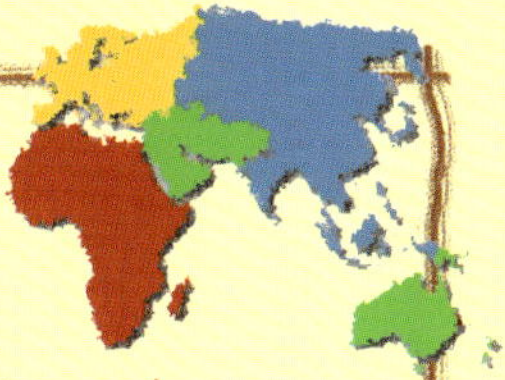

Following

Mary and Joseph were not the only ones travelling in the days before Jesus was born. Some wise men had left the security of their homes and had begun following the star that would lead them to Bethlehem. They travelled a long way from the east so that they could see the new-born 'King of the Jews' and join in the celebration of Jesus' birth.

Advent is . . .

Showing

The Bible tells us that a bright star came to rest over the place where Jesus was born. It was a very special sign, showing where the new King was.

Although, compared to the sun, a star only gives a little light, it was enough to bring the wise men to Jesus. It teaches us that sometimes we have to trust the little light that we have to find our own way to Jesus.

Advent is . . .

Searching

Even before Jesus was born, people were looking for him. The prophets foresaw the coming of the Messiah, and others searched the scriptures for clues. Some, like the wise men, searched for him by asking questions. They thought Jesus would be born in a palace and visited King Herod to ask where he was. They did not yet know that those who find Jesus do so because God reveals him.

Advent is . . .

Journeying

Mary and Joseph had to travel a long way to get to Bethlehem from their home in Nazareth.

Mary was *about* to have a *baby*, and *so* rode on a donkey rather than walk.

The *seventy-mile* journey would have *taken about* ten days.

Advent is . . .

Welcoming

When Mary and Joseph arrived at Bethlehem they were tired and needed somewhere to stay. The inn was full. However, the innkeeper did not turn them away, but found room for them in a stable.

Advent is a time for remembering that we too have to welcome and make room for Jesus.

Advent is . . .

Interpreting

Year after year during Advent we tell the stories of Jesus' birth as they are told in the Gospels. We bring the stories to life in school Nativity plays and in Christmas presentations. But what we tell is more than a story; it is a set of clues about where God is to be found in the world. God is there in the manger, in the poverty, in the places where people are hurt and rejected and left out.

Advent is . . .

Astounding

A story in the Old Testament tells how God took Moses to the top of a mountain and showed him the promised land. Advent is like standing on that mountain with Moses, but instead of seeing the promised land, we glimpse what God's kingdom will be like. It will be a place where the broken are made whole and the wounded are healed, where God's love is in everything and means everything.

Advent is . . .

Announcing

Advent is a time for angels, the messengers of God. An angel told both Elizabeth and Mary that they were with child and an angel came to reassure Zechariah and Joseph, the fathers of John and Jesus, that there was nothing to fear. It was angels that formed the heavenly choir when Jesus was born; and it was angels that announced the Good News to the shepherds.

Advent is . . .

Celebrating

During Advent people gather together to sing. Sometimes a group of people will go from door to door, singing carols and collecting gifts of money for those in need. Carols celebrate the coming of Christmas, but they are also a rehearsal for the choir that will welcome Jesus when as the Bridegroom he comes to meet the Church, his bride.

Advent is . . .

Worshipping

When Jesus was born the Magi came from far away to worship him. They knew how special he was, and brought special gifts. Gold they brought for a king, incense for a priest, myrrh for a burial. Each gift, whether they knew it or not, anticipated a part of Jesus' life. Jesus is worshipped as the heavenly King, the great High Priest, and the dying and rising Lord.

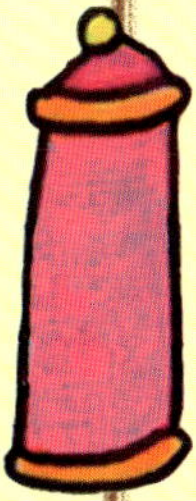

Advent is . . .

Giving

During Advent gifts are wrapped
to give on Christmas Day.
They are signs of love and care.
It is very exciting to open them up
to see what is inside.

God's greatest gift to us is Jesus.
The Bible teaches us that God loved us so
much that he gave us Jesus, and if we
believe in him, we will live for ever with God.

Advent is . . .

Arriving

The season of Advent ends
at midnight on Christmas Eve when
the white candle on the Advent Wreath
is lit, and all creation sings to
proclaim the Messiah's birth.
This is the end of our Advent journey,
but not the last word.
Jesus said; 'I am coming soon.'

'Amen. Come, Lord Jesus.'

Advent is . . .

Disturbing

Herod, the King of the Jews, was very disturbed when he heard that a new 'King of the Jews' was to be born: he did not want anything to change. He was right to be worried, because when Jesus comes to reign he will divide those who are good from those who are evil, and he will reward the good and punish the evil, and Herod was an evil man.

First published in 2007 by

KEVIN MAYHEW LTD
Buxhall, Stowmarket, Suffolk, IP14 3BW
E-mail: info@kevinmayhewltd.com
Website: www.kevinmayhew.com

9 8 7 6 5 4 3 2 1 0

ISBN 978 1 84417 806 3
Catalogue No. 1501033

Illustrations by George & Angie Allen
Design by Chris Coe

Printed and bound in EU